Also by Naomi Lazard:

Cry of the Peacocks
The Moonlit Upper Deckerina

Naomi Lazard

ORDINANCES

ARDIS / ANN ARBOR

Naomi Lazard

Ordinances

Copyright © 1978 by Naomi Lazard

ISBN 0-88233-256-2 (cloth)
ISBN 0-88233-257-0 (paperbound)

Published by Ardis,
2901 Heatherway,
Ann Arbor, Michigan, 48104

Cover by Naomi Lazard and Ellendea Proffer

ACKNOWLEDGMENTS

The author gratefully acknowledges the help
of a Fels Award and CAPS Grant.

Special thanks also to Greenwich Fine Arts, Inc.
Greenwich, Conn.

These poems originally appeared in the following pub-
lications: *Big Moon:* Ordinance on Meeting; *Harper's Mag-
azine:* Ordinance on Lining Up, Ordinance on Enrollment, Ordi-
nance on the News from the Front, Re Accepting You, Ordinance
on Existence, Ordinance at the Level Crossing; *The Nation:* Or-
dinance on Getting Better, Ordinance on Miracles, Rooftop Or-
dinance, Ordinance on Winning; *The Ohio Review:* The Beast's
Ordinance, Ordinance on Employment, Ordinance on the Compe-
tition, Ordinance on a Building Site, In Answer to Your Query,
Ordinance on Failure; *The Ontario Review:* Ordinance on Arrival;
The Paris Review: Ordinance on Citation (under the title "The
Citation"), Grand Opening, Public Notice; *Varlik:* Ordinance on
the News from the Front (translated by Talat Sait Halman).

This poetry is a winner of a di Castagnola award of the
Poetry Society of America.

CONTENTS

This book is for my sister, Myrna

ORDINANCES

ORDINANCE ON ARRIVAL■■■■■■■■■■■■■■■■■■■■■■

Welcome to you
who have managed to get here.
It's been a terrible trip;
you should be happy you have survived it.
Statistics prove that not many do.
You would like a bath, a hot meal,
a good night's sleep. Some of you
need medical attention.
None of this is available.
These things have always been
in short supply; now
they are impossible to obtain.

      This is not
a temporary situation;
it is permanent.
Our condolences on your disappointment.
It is not our responsibility
everything you have heard about this place
is false. It is not our fault
you have been deceived,
ruined your health getting here.
For reasons beyond our control
there is no vehicle out.

THE BEAST'S ORDINANCE ■■■■■■■■■■■■■■■■■■■■■

When you pass through this door
don't leave your spirit outside
like an umbrella in the hallway.
Step over the threshold
into the space provided for you.
If you feel dissatisfied
with this space, there is the window;
you may jump out.
If you are not that dissatisfied
find the most comfortable spot
and lower yourself into it.
Temperature controls are handy
for heat and air-conditioning.
There is plenty of food
in the refrigerator. The bed
is comfortable, with an orthopedic
mattress. The table is set for eight
in case you want to have people for dinner
The bookcases are filled with books
you might have chosen yourself.
The carpets are thick;
noise is at a minimum.
The walls are covered
with attractive lithographs and prints.
Clean towels are always available;
also sheets and pillowcases
in the latest no-iron patterns.
Everything important is provided.

Someone is close by
who will be just like a lover to you.
Someone else,
just like a friend.

This job is not for bums or drop-outs.
Slacking off is not permitted.
We took you on
in spite of our better judgment;
papers were signed, notarized.
You had time to reconsider;
now it is too late.
The work in progress must continue.
You are essential to its completion.

It is not our responsibility
that you don't like your co-workers
and they don't like you.
Nobody is here to be liked.
You must do the best you can
under the circumstances.
We try to make them better for you.
The experimentation chamber
is being moved to another building;
you should no longer be distracted
by the sounds produced there.
The conveyer belts are scheduled
for upholstering; color and fabric
were chosen by a top flight designer.
Ventilator shafts have been refurbished;
lethal fumes are a thing of the past.
Outmoded tile in all receiving rooms
is being replaced with marble.

On order is a new vulture proof plastic
for the disposal of carrion.
There is a spiritual adviser;
he is efficient and helpful.
The zoo is being restocked
with friendlier animals.

Many people think of you as fortunate
even though you now find the work distasteful.
We have our own problems,
working round the clock
to keep things going.

The signs indicate
that you are getting much better.
For example, you are not nearly as prone
to feeling abandoned
when friends don't telephone
for weeks on end. You understand
their delinquency has nothing to do
with the bond between you.
It doesn't mean anything definite
about your character. You know
it is not a judgment; they have not
found you out. Your suffering,
these days, is not grand opera.
You have changed enormously.

A good case in point:
only this morning you noticed
half your face was missing.
It is significant that you were able
to remark to yourself
how many people live decently
with half a face. You might remember
that just a short time ago
you would have been distraught
at such an occurrence. Now
you appreciate your gifts,
nor do you label as crazy
the people who want to be close to you.

This is all because you are better.

You must not be distracted
by your dreams. It doesn't matter
that in your dreams
trains pull away just as you reach
the platform, that swimmers
strike out for the open sea
without you. Try to forget
that house in your dreams,
the light bulb hanging
in the room you live in,
and the newspapers which cover the windows.

Nobody loves a miracle more than we do.
This life falls so short
of your expectations;
it is so filled with frustration,
hopelessness, even despair.
More people than ever before
are talking to themselves
in public places.

Therefore we accept miracles
as an adjunct to your spiritual well-being.
We consider miracles necessary
in order to fill certain vacuums.
If a miracle happens to you
don't try to keep it private;
telephone your friends
even though some of them may be scoffers.
You yourself know best
the seemingly impossible change in your life,
as if it had been suddenly sweetened.
The scoffers will advise you
to be wary of everything, to be skeptical.
We advise this too, but we don't insist.
We want to help you all we can
to enjoy life to its fullest.

We understand your life is bleak,
that it drones on.

The dismal humming you hear
is the sound it usually makes.
A miracle can step up the gear,
change the sound into something else.

Enjoy your miracle
however long it lasts,
however momentary. Remember,
when it is over
your life slows down considerably
and sometimes grinds to a halt.

We are happy to inform you
your achievement has been recognized.
After having spent your life
on this endeavor, after the sacrifices
you have made, you must be pleased
by the outcome. We are too.
It is our pleasant duty
to strike the medallion
commemorating your success.
We hope it is everything
you ever wanted in a medallion.
Its value is not
in the materials it is made of,
but in its meaning;
the tribute to your merit.
We hope you will be proud of it,
consider it a work of art as well,
remember the craftsmanship
that went into it
despite its small size.
We would also like to offer
our whole hearted support
on your future projects.
You obviously richly deserve it.

Coda:
        The medallion
must never be shown or worn.

Our correspondence closes
with this letter.

ORDINANCE AT THE LEVEL CROSSING ■■■■■■■■■

Jumping the track is forbidden;
the penalty for offenders is death.
You are permitted
to live beside the track,
work at your trade,
take trips, raise your family—
but always on this side.

It will not be considered an excuse
that trains don't run here anymore.
They used to run here
and they may again.
The Council is having a heated debate
on whether to allow trains.
All factors are being taken into consideration.
The faction that definitely opposes
trains running here again
says the situation is dangerous enough
at present. Actual trains
will constitute an intolerable risk
to life and property.
Their argument is:
under present conditions
the danger is contained.
The faction favoring trains
proposes a modified run
of no more than two a year.

The progress of this debate
will be reported from time to time
as we see fit.

Follow the arrows to the viewing hall.
The time you are allowed there:
five minutes from the moment you enter.
The rules:
             You may stand still
or walk; under no circumstances
may you speak to anyone, not even a guard.
Whispering disqualifies you.
No smoking. No spitting.

To help you
here is a list
regarding the object displayed.
The valves projecting sidewise curve upward,
not for decoration, but because
of internal necessity. The topmost duct,
just below the grinder, emits a fluid
which is not dangerous.
It may be inhaled but not tasted.
The protrusion which appears to be a hump
is red hot to the touch.
The conical shape on which the object rests
lights up periodically. This aura
is similar to radiation though low in intensity,
well within the limits of safe dosage.
The crooked edge is filed to razor sharpness;
do not run your hand along it.
The grunting sound you may hear

is caused by the gears shifting.
The sparks flying out from time to time
must be considered in context.

The above message has been printed
for your safety and convenience.
All visitors and contestants
are invited inside at their own risk.
Each person is allowed one guess
as to the purpose of the object.
The first one to answer correctly
will be the winner.
                    The prize
is the object itself which will be delivered,
free of charge, to home or office.

This card certifies the following:
your file was processed,
found satisfactory, the number
of counts against you
counterbalanced by favorable ones.

A few words regarding your card:
it is the product of years
of intense survey, research
requiring judgments concerning
data on the entire population.
Despite the many obstacles
we forged ahead; now we take pride
in our achievement. This card
eliminates waste and effort.
Things will go more smoothly for you;
there will be less chance of delay
caused by mishaps, forgetfulness
or misunderstanding.
No other form of identification
will ever be needed.
Those to whom you show this card
will know you exist
without further confirmation.

Notice:
          Our experts have devised a system
unlike any other. You do not have

just another number here.
The small microprint on the reverse side
contains enough information
to satisfy the most severe questioner.
                    Everyone qualified
will soon be equipped with the device
to interpret the code.

Flash this card.
It is all you need.

This showroom is now open.
You will see the most complete collection
of debris fashioned into the necessary shapes.
Current trends
have been taken into consideration.
Each shape consists of parts
made of heavy gauge metal;
all parts, moving or otherwise,
are soldered into place,
not merely pasted or pinned.
This feature is the well known bonus
distinguishing our product
from its imitators.

The recent ruling
regards the acquisition of an article
such as the ones on exhibition.
Come in immediately.
Reserve yours; you may pay for it later
with any of the major credit cards.

A brief summary:
From the specified date
you must in some manner
carry wherever you go
a shape made of metal
of the ordained weight and size.
This shape need not be fastened

to your body; it may be carried or lugged
behind. It must be with you at all times.
If you prefer
you may carry it on the back of a truck,
shackle it to your car,
or put it into a hand-cart.
For those of you who use a bicycle
or are still too young even for that,
we have a line of sleds
which can be pulled by a rope.

This ramp is not a pedestrian walk.
Violators will be disciplined.
This ramp is the fruit
of highly skilled, specialized research;
designed only for appropriate vehicles.
Nothing and no one with legs
permitted here for any reason
whatsoever. The impact caused by feet,
especially in shoes, would be disastrous
to its performance. Disciplinary
action will be prompt and severe.
Offenders will be prosecuted
without regard for age or sex.
This ramp is one of several
in an experimental project,
the first anywhere. It has been given
the Better Government Seal of Approval.
We expect that in the very near future
many more will be installed.
Orders are coming in
at a rate we honestly did not anticipate.
The vehicles are scheduled
for production; plants requisitioned,
converted to that purpose.
This project will go forward
as quickly as possible.
We are doing our best to fill orders
for both ramps and vehicles
as fast as they come in.

ORDINANCE ON A BUILDING SITE ■■■■■■■■■■■■■■

This wall is painted
a particular shade of grey
which is peaceful; the building
on the lot behind it has been demolished.
A new one is going up.
                                This site
was chosen from a group
generously offered by benefactors
who prefer to remain anonymous.
It is a perfect site for the purpose.

Notes on the new building:
Its appearance need not startle you;
at one time turrets were commonplace.
These are different only
in the fact they rotate.
A previous unknown, cellular material,
which performs in the same manner as lungs
is the substitution for windows.
The overhang will serve
as a sunshade in summer
for the entire community.
An organic substance
used in the construction of the walls
accounts for the expansion and contraction;
the building changes form
regularly but slightly.
The missing entrance is easily explained:

egress to the building will be across the street,
then down through a tunnel
leading directly to the lower levels.

Caution:
         No leaning against this wall.
Absolutely no graffiti.
No talking to the workmen;
you can recognize them by the rubber masks.

RE ACCEPTING YOU ■■■■■■■■■■■■■■■■■■■■■■■■■■■■■

We are very pleased with your response
to our advertisement. The form
you found in which to couch your reply
is original and attractive.
It caught our attention immediately.
The fact that you did not wait,
but answered at once, is also
in your favor. This means
you are a decisive person,
and this is the type we are looking for.
So many people, these days,
are trapped in indecision.
We agree profoundly with everything
you have said. More than anything
we agree with the way you have said it.

You seem to have understood
that the person we need must be humorous.
That, we assure you, is a prime factor.
You have told us a great deal
about yourself, and the telling
was brief. This too is a virtue.
We like it. Lastly,
you appear not to have become bitter
from your experience. This
we find extraordinary.

At this point we would like to meet you.

You are invited to come here
for an evening we have arranged.
Everyone to whom we have written
favorable answers such as this one
will be here. You will come
at your own expense. The trip
will be worth the trouble. The party,
as long as it lasts, will be fun.
If things don't work out as you hope
you will not be reimbursed,
but you will be placed
on our mailing list.

ORDINANCE ON LINING UP ■■■■■■■■■■■■■■■■■■■■■

A line will form to the right
and one to the left. You must join
one of them. After careful consideration
choose the line you are most attracted to;
stand at the end of it.
Both lines are serpentine. However,
if you look closely
you will see subtle differences.
The one to the right moves more quickly,
the left line at a more leisurely pace
which may prove beneficial
to certain dispositions.

Try to see where the lines go;
this is your option.
Everything possible is being done
to protect your privileges.
A factor to keep in mind:
in joining the line to the right
you will end life as a beggar.
If you decide on the line to the left
everything you believe will become nonsense.
You will be spending
a great deal of time on whichever one
you choose. Choose wisely.
No changing from one line to the other
once you have joined.
                       Common sense

will tell you that you will become
an indispensable link
in the line of your choice.

                    Good luck to you.

ORDINANCE ON MEETING ■■■■■■■■■■■■■■■■■■■■■

If you must meet
wait until the train
has pulled out of the station;
now you can't get off.
Walk against the movement of the train
to the last car. You may meet there.
One of you will see the other first.
The one seeing waits
to be noticed. The one seen
turns suddenly, embarrassed.
He stammers, "I meant to call you,"
or, "I've been so busy."
The first one knows now
the meeting was a mistake.
This will not prevent another one
on this train or somewhere else
where the rules, of course,
are the same.

IN ANSWER TO YOUR QUERY∎∎∎∎∎∎∎∎∎∎∎∎∎∎∎∎∎∎

We are sorry to inform you
the item you ordered
is no longer being produced.
It has not gone out of style
nor have people lost interest in it.
In fact, it has become
one of our most desired products.
Its popularity is still growing.
Orders for it come in
at an ever increasing rate.
However, a top-level decision
has caused this product
to be discontinued forever.

Instead of the item you ordered
we are sending you something else.
It is not the same thing,
nor is it a reasonable facsimile.
It is what we have in stock,
the very best we can offer.

If you are not happy
with this substitution
let us know as soon as possible.
                As you can imagine
we already have quite an accumulation
of letters such as the one
you may or may not write.

To be totally fair
we respond to these complaints
as they come in.
Yours will be filed accordingly,
answered in its turn.

ROOFTOP ORDINANCE ■■■■■■■■■■■■■■■■■■■■■■■■■

You are one of the lucky inhabitants
of this building. As you know
it is the finest building of its type,
designed by an internationally famous
architect, built by an equally prestigious
construction firm. Its concept and planning
were years in the works.
                                    This is also
the world's tallest building.
Precautions are necessary
when you use the roof.
Do not over-exert yourself:
walk out upon it as slowly as you can,
then sit down or better still
lower yourself to a prone position.
If you have a medical history
see your physician beforehand.
He will advise you
regarding your safe exposure.
You will learn to find the roof enjoyable
if you follow instructions.

Notice:
            The roof has been transformed
into a garden for your pleasure.
No effort has been stinted
on the landscaping. You must resign yourself
to the vertigo; there was nothing

we could do about the motion of the earth.
Keep your eyes on your happy neighbors
reclining in the chairs provided,
spinning gaily, lurching in the wind.

The group in process of being formed
will be something you have always wanted
to be a part of but never, heretofore,
imagined possible. Its composition
will be strictly regulated:
only those who qualify will be admitted.
All others will be rejected.
For those of you who believe
you may have the necessary attributes
for entry into this group
an application can be picked up
at our office. Answer the questions
as honestly as you can. Good marks
also given for imagination
and resourcefulness. This group,
as it is shaping up, promises
to become a compelling force
in our society.
                    If you fail
to get into this group
another, larger group is also being formed
for rejects from the first one.
The second group will in no way
be inferior to the first. It too
has standards; they are high.
In order for your application
to permit entry into the second group
check the proper place.

In case the second group is filled
before your application can be processed,
or your qualifications fall short,
do not be despondent. Our plans include
the formation of a third group.
All applicants who have failed
to make it into the first or second groups
will automatically qualify for the third.
This is not to imply that standards
for this section are not high.
They are different.
                          We welcome you now
to the group for which you will ultimately
qualify. Whichever it is
we know you will have a creative
and enriching experience.

SPACE FUN ■■■■■■■■■■■■■■■■■■■■■■■■■■■■■■■■■■■

For your trip into the stratosphere
here are the types of vessels;
a capsule shaped like a bottle
with an interesting cap
of simulated lead crystal;
one that is reminiscent of a raft,
laminated in driftwood finish;
the show stopper, cylindrical,
based on the idea of a test tube.
Its hatch is disguised
as a bunsen burner.

All the vessels
are constructed according
to the latest, most severe standards
of safety and comfort.
This is important.
You will be living in the vessel
you choose for a long time.

Reports of the danger
involved in the voyage
are grossly exaggerated.
Follow the simple instructions
in your manual;
you should arrive at your destination
without mishap.
                    In the event

you do not reach your destination,
the pleasures of indefinite travel
through space will be enhanced.

These distinctive, charming crafts
are at a premium. Buy yours
while they last. Everyone will need one
in order to make the journey.
Act quickly.
Bon voyage!

ORDINANCE ON THE NEWS FROM THE FRONT ■■

All the reports that have reached you
are true. In that area known as the front
no one sleeps anymore.
According to a recent bulletin
we know that infants are born there
with their eyes open; chickens
stagger in the dusty roads
for lack of sleep. There is
no escaping the disasters,
nor is there any chance for a settlement.
Nobody knows how it will all end.

However, we are doing all we can
to limit the conflict, and, if possible,
to stop it. Our efforts to date
have been successful. The war
is contained in a small area, the front.

The rumor that this front is advancing
is not true. It is common knowledge
that the front is elsewhere,
in another country.
We are keeping it there
where it belongs.

Congratulations.
The suspense is over. You are the winner.
The doubts you have had
concerning the rules of the contest,
about the ability and fairness of the judges,
were illfounded. The rumors
pertaining to a "fix"
have been exposed as nonsense.
The contest is fair and always has been.
Now that the results are in
your prize will be sent to you
under separate cover. Be sure to have
your social security number
or other proper identification
for the postman.
                     Upon receiving it
contact us immediately
in order that you may be notified
of further developments, ensuing publicity,
other honors which will be forthcoming.
If by some chance your prize does not arrive
as scheduled, do not bother to inform us.

Our responsibility is discharged
with this announcement.
In the event that you do not receive
your prize, there is no authority
to whom you can turn

for information or redress.
We advise you to wait patiently
for your prize
which will either come or not.

ORDINANCE ON FAILURE ■■■■■■■■■■■■■■■■■■■■■■

Now that you have lost
there is no going back to start again
no matter how much you would like to.
We do not operate a time machine,
cannot take on the repair
of what has already happened.
It is official.
Everyone knows about it or soon will.
We could say
this is an extraordinary situation
for you, but we cannot.
Unfortunately
it is all too ordinary.
Come to terms, as best you can,
with the facts. After what
you have been through
don't despise yourself now
any more than is necessary.
Nobody knows better than we do
how you have struggled
for a bit of the precipice.
Sympathy is in order;
there is nothing we can do.
You are a failure. There it is.
We continue to do our utmost
to find the solution to this problem.
The best minds at our disposal
are working in closed session.

You can imagine the difficulties.
Each failure is unique;
sui generis is the term for it.
Reflect on this.
The comfort you find in its truth
will sustain you.

ORDINANCE ON DEPARTURE ■■■■■■■■■■■■■■■■■

When the time comes to leave
you will know it at once.
The signal is unmistakable.
It will be of no help
to find out when the others leave.
Your signal is in a special key
finely tuned to your ears alone.
Try not to be agitated
by the signals belonging
to the departure of others.
It is hard enough work
straining to hear your own signal.
Once you hear it
you won't have much time.
Recently
the time given between your signal
and subsequent departure
has been cut drastically.
This cut has been necessary
because of the crisis.
It was inevitable.
You will have ten seconds
after you identify your signal.

Warning:
        There is a difference
between arriving and leaving
even though occasionally

someone arrives walking backwards
and viceversa. Most of the time
everyone enters or leaves
facing the right direction.